songbird

~ *wesleyan poetry*

song bird

CAROL ANN DAVIS

wesleyan university press
middletown connecticut

Wesleyan University Press
Middletown CT 06459
www.wesleyan.edu/wespress

Manufactured in the
United States of America
Designed and composed in Arno Pro
by Eric M. Brooks

Library of Congress
Cataloging-in-Publication Data
NAMES: Davis, Carol Ann, 1970– author.
TITLE: Songbird / Carol Ann Davis.
DESCRIPTION: First. | Middletown, Connecticut : Wesleyan University Press, 2026. |
SERIES: Wesleyan poetry | Summary: "A sequence of short lyric poems addressing the urgent and ancient passage from child to adult, finding both the sensuous and the sacred, and invoking what it means to open the mouth and sing" — Provided by publisher.
IDENTIFIERS: LCCN 2025035015 (print) | LCCN 2025035016 (ebook) |
ISBN 9780819502216 paperback | ISBN 9780819502223 ebook
SUBJECTS: LCGFT: Lyric poetry
CLASSIFICATION: LCC PS3604.A95578 S66 2026 (print) |
LCC PS3604.A95578 (ebook)
LC record available at https://lccn.loc.gov/2025035015
LC ebook record available at https://lccn.loc.gov/2025035016

5 4 3 2 1

One day when the bluebells were in bloom I wrote the following.

GERARD MANLEY HOPKINS

contents

~ up from spine these grasses

come to shush belly-low the song
spine of which in proper translation of god-head
languages into evensong my way of taking off what it means
to be in a body yet body-wise I'm spine and in these grasses
I'm also field that appears when I become quiet
to have been alive when I was dead no matter
the world's here to shush me sky is shushing
and luscious smell of what was it they called *linseed*
on the pew railing its shush that says *too much* and me too much
until someone explains how to keep day from coming
but day is here day is lowing the sun from darkness sure
but also the big argument about all the words one can use
for *indulgence* the myriad theologies at play behind *works* and *deeds*
not heavy robes but cotton not ornament but its spare-bred opposite
in a plain light to ask after *like* and *if* as if by analogy

to arrive at *bones*   which are *bread*   and *blood* which is *wine*

yet I'm the cartilege of the smalls   of first questions

the formation   of which   I'm just now aware   but was I ever

young   you tell me   who seems   to have run

soft over my peeling shoulders   with devotion   to have

inventoried daily   the freckles formed   *in* or *by* my quiet

over and over they say   *she's too quiet*   yet about me already

there's water   cookies with flour   and the oil from the pew

everything yes everything   that can spill from me   is spilling

and all i say's apology   a totality in shushing sun   till who was it

won't i find   who said to me   prophet girl   everything's a song

if you choose   from lowdown in the belly   if you pull   up from spine

you'll see   every bit of it   even the sky wants   cries out   for you to moan

~ let me take something small

between my teeth

piece of straw meant to signify your body

which was given freely to me or threads of me

that are wheat strands always these small barters

for a price would I give you the edge that is

your absence for my presence and you between my teeth

for the price of grass the price of all grasses

so say I to you in prayer I would

swallow whole what gave you in part

~ what gave you in part

its body to be burned

room I enter by my own burning

what of my calciums and your beauty

from cups a calculus of mist

multiplied by rust cup of mornings

among evensong running over

and your voice the calling hymn

did you say *as ocean to deep* my name

did I resemble *the silver*

water of dusk a silver in the mouth

by my own burning you open to swallow me

~ by my own burning do you

open to swallow me

dross of my body laid   by god-claim same

as dross god-spit-out   each issued

from my plus-minus mouth   to announce

world is chalk-made   world is dust

by what burns in us   to make our sustenance

you from my burning   take your tax

and by my blooms   be you marked

so let shine   your infinities

on my tongue

~ let shine your infinities

on my tongue

by my own shining   unweave me

then by authority   of your milk thistle stitch

weave me back   to my cottons

that innermost   catch and click

after all   by what shining   do you know yourself

if not in part by me   that takes you whole

into my mouth   restless part that blooms

with the thought   of me somewhere

and my cotton unwoven

~ me somewhere

and my cotton unwoven

comes to you late   or already born

still it makes   or makes itself over

in likeness   you'd cottoned to

me somewhere in silks   you'd not willingly

in linens and skins   thought chalk

thought riverine   somewhere in which

you lay a blanket down   or I do as in

the unweaving a wing does   to the air

the unfurling of the wave   down the ocean's

long throat   there on the blanket

your honey   its gathers temporary

fresh fruit of you   to pull the mouth close

~ temporary

the fresh fruit of you

which pulls the mouth close   and with it all color

the tongue blind   to aftertaste of *is*

and back from   all my given edges

light light of daybreak   morning fog

temporary as *if wishes   were horses*

though I'd beg to ride   and do in my way beg

but far fresher   want made new   by your gaze

by the not-said said   that fills the air

fresh as the lemon scent   on the hands

o what did I touch   that took me so

~ you in your molt

and me in mine

that you might see it I let the vein darken

instead with a finger you show me

the spalt in the wood my admixture heavy

with the rhume of your particular both of us open

where the air would darken us so let the vein darken

into this our thin skin and rising there the moon

you in your molt me naked but for

your spalt and your dross

~ me naked but for

your spalt

me alone but for   your dross

hungry except   the tidy morsel

of your body moving   me eye-fed but for

what remains hidden   the underwing and lash

what are the rumors   and where is sunshine

what comes to us   after that blinding

me blind but for   what I could touch

me touched but for   where I wouldn't

what was this nakedness   I kept for you

cloth I wove and unwove   so that it covered

what you couldn't

~ cloth I wove and unwove

so that covered

over waxes unwoven   as seine net in shallows

empties itself   of all knowns   cloth I kept close

and cast out   what *seemed* from what *is*

or were you the membrane   closing me from myself

the wove-unwove that   might otherwise slip

like fish in shallows   the knot of netting

its translucent strings   which move us

in dawn light   from stuff of sleep   to stuff of waking

the work the body does   to weave itself

and you there stirring   by all emptiness could I

hold there my shallows

~ by all emptiness

could I hold you there

my shallows small   in my particular

and you threadbare   could I hold anything

in these bony fingers   and for any long-mattering

by my attention find you   earth-bound   earth-arrowing

among deep   and departing sugars   no

in this new-yellowing fall   you're air-made

and disappearing   a scent on my hands

an oil-slick in the air   as if creation depended

entirely on absences   that accrue

~ entirely from absences

that accrue

I make my enamels   entirely from dross

of silence and rust   my calcium forms

and from shapes composed   by sleep

my waking's made   entirely of shipwreck

a loose joinery   of mortise and tenon

attends my apart-coming   yellow leaves

slow-passing   the heart of the matter

and from matter slipping   through the hands

your hair   the oils   of your fingertips

entirely by the stuff   of your touch

is my waking made   as when you woke

and I imagined the sun   your face

~ and imagined the sun

your face

imagined the curve of the earth   and bowls

the oceans make   each of our disappearing

imagined the sum   of all particulates

of dust and of clouds   imagined the tongue

and you here   eyes that close and open

hands that touch   imagined touch as birdsong

and windsong   imagined all else

as what it was   and tried to see it

as yellow leaves slow   in slow motion

the wet ground   that waits for them

fell me slowly then   into the unending

as if you could answer   yes

~ into the unending

                                        as if you could answer

yes   fell most of my knowing

into the sound of stream-fed   and feeding

the *yes*   of what distances water falls

to be here on our faces   and our faces

upward to sky   falling forward

a grief's vertigo   and balance

the way yellowing   the leaves supplicate

as if to answer   cloud-gather

or answering's the way   they move

their shapely bodies   as we move ours

in prayer   yes   falls most

of my knowing   into the mouth

of all   that would swallow me

~ of all that would swallow me

what is written

and where is it written   that our swallows arrow

anywhere but up and up   till in cloud-mist they find

how we were before   cell by cell we separate

what's recorded of mouths   before they open

the light-sensing we did   before orbs of eyes

or concept of opening   the *aware* before aware

when world was seam   fault   and vein

of crevasse in me   a single verse is recorded

and of you almost nothing   except that

I touched my hand   to the cave wall

and came away   covered in sky

~ and came away

covered in sky

and slipped thinnest   into made-sky

say what it is   you want said sky   made deep

by its own bluing   *uncover what cloaks*

not by this naysaying   my own atmosphere

turned to me   my made-of-nothing

slipped minor key   down throat of instrument

as bluing overtook   and what gave

my nakedness   its lowing sound showed

the milk its river   the cloud its bodying ash

as if what held me   to my body

also held me   by thin string to you

~ also by thin string

did you answer

my bitter   with your salt   my glove

your hammer   and nail your hand

also by string pulled tight   did you ease me

down where melody cracks   its dry wood

regret to devotion   by such a string as this

the egg its yellow yolk   was I made to vibrate

and by your fingers   do I climb nearer

gather you by the fistful   and look

how you flower   in my hands if I let you

~ and look how you flower

in my hands if I let you

look how we spin like petals in water

our shape mirrored by vein and current

in the purity of that which ribbons easily

out of you toward where I've been waiting

look how my asking resembles

the blue of holy paintings where the boy

holds the ball out to someone unseen

and brushstroke's meant to string lengthwise

us along the earth's axis look at me thus

as if I were paint and with one finger

scrape a piece of me by way of looking-prayer

lift me lift me into your mouth

~ by way of looking-prayer

lift me as the world does

then return me wholesale   my shortcomings in ash

how soon   we come to it   the charcoal outline

bullet fragmenting bone   or mouth of river

that holds inside it   all our endings

you with the rope   and the steady beam

Celan with that high spiraling   staircase

it turns out the world   is full

of instruments of torture   my own teeth

tongue I was given   and my unsteady hand

along with its acids   what if my heart is ash

and by my touch   do I bring you ruin

~ by my touch

do I bring ruin

rain comes down   from my acid cloud

and from my keening issues   a faint poison gas

is my striated doubt enough   to stop waking though

the sunlight comes for you   or is that me shining

through a window   sashed with a death-bringing

all my own   love have I   claimed the milk

in the river   along with oil in same   and by my saming

have I twinned   the signal fire that was

all wanting   to its paltry smoke

have I just by looking   loosed my bluing

or does my name with it   go wanting

~ does my name go wanting

by such brightnesses as vision

does my dark poison make itself over into blankets and rust

what song would it be in which my note's not flat

bearing terrors that visit unnamed but purchased

what's the half-measure that takes the sting from the blood

bud from its frost how from these ancient parts

does petal unfold into nothing but

a glancing possibility please find please visit me

who sees after all my thin-sheet covering

o put me put me there where I still

spin in the light

~ there where I still

spin in the light

the cobalt and coal   of my contours blur

till blur is   my name in your mouth

and tongue same   there where my scent

would daydream you back   say into or out of

our thousand worries   there do I take you

where my hand rested   and who was it

that put it there   so much translucence

or perhaps it's light   makes of itself

as I do you   mirror read

as breath reads fog

~ read me please

as breath reads fog

take as fragment   my threadbare rest

burn whole and pour out   what's become of me

onto clean white paper   pour what the ashes say

detect with your supersonic   blue flower spectrum

run along baseboard   at last known address

and when all's lost   let the bloodhounds come

along with the fresco-painters   and readers of braille

mix with mortar and pestle   that in me which begs

to become powder   taste at last   those parts of me

I never offered   by my endings make of me

a scent on the hands   lemon or poppy

impossible to name

~ o *lemon or poppy*

impossible to name

by whose scent do you touch me

in what space does my body come to rest

so you're zip-code near my out-breath your in-

by what accident did my birth year brush

close to yours and by documentary

what trace you into almanacs record books

or surviving film a lone scratchy recording

brings throughline of you as you were

to me as now how then to touch

with modern hands all you my ancients

or reach me on my island's misunderstanding

how correct me of impression

you just left the air I am touching

~ that you just left

the air I am touching

definite as the proposition a blue salvia's

July nectar to starving flyers

it's undisputed truth that I claw at emptiness

the way straight seeks round and a thousand other

postulates for the geometry of our coming and going

the riven calculus already proven of our plus

and minus and nothing found in nature

bubbles in the blood the way your blue veins quicken

undetected except where I brush a finger

along the wrist accidental as the certainty

you ever lived under same incalculable sky

or held me temporary as any joining

in your arms

~ something as temporary

as our joining

gnawed bone and teeth look how

seconds accrue as you make of me me

before molecules reconstitute into half-wing

on saucer yet you were here to see

the orbs of my eyes in utero before that

your footstep like first feathers

I gathered to me you were moon-dust

day I stretched my arms to swim free

in the ocean's deep you don't remember me

first time you ever but right as rain

those were my wind-fingers in your hair

~ those were my wind-fingers

in your hair

up and up into atmosphere   swirling with postulates

and pencil-dark my spinning   where you slipped

your nothing   then lit   with your eyes a last match

that was my sandstorm   smoke-screen

and wet blanket anytime   your pigment blushed

or mine did   that was the pressure   of your fingertips

on me fragmentary   dust-made and prone

swept clean as air   and you the air

burning in lungs   whence came the blood

of all my bluing

~ whence came the blood

of all my bluing

and who was born to me who counted my calciums

or felt my silver kisses cell to cell my skin

grafted onto imaginings and no vines to twin me

except the both of us unborn my nub of milkweed

your minor third by roadside how could I answer you

except to eat the bark of that tree

and finally admit all the world is seed

and you its water

~ if all the world is seed

and you its water

then underbloom's fortune's   tied permanently

to rampart   and ruin's sewn

inside every psalm   if the hymnody's rent

by ratio of thees   to thines

our own given ratio   in your palm notebook

serves definitive proof   of maker's mark on clay

if your touch here   on my wrist were tattoo

and your water's my spending   allotted to thirst

equal parts doubt   and prayer   then might we

this once   open our mouths

and drink

~ to open our mouths

and drink

under weight to bear up   allow fissure comb

up and up where nothing   so much as glances

a branch but loosens   to let fruit-heavy fall

to let runneth over   goodness cupped

by its opposite   burn burnish and mark

that which hinges   join without nailing

and find vein by touch   place an inky *x*

light the fuse   call from birth our claim

own   and set spinning the spell

that calls our tidy name

~ set spinning the spell

that tidy calls

my fine ribbons of being   worship at feet

of foot soldiers   slake the forsaken

take on what waters   aloe what burns

split with fingernail   what the sun blisters

and by our tidy naming   let planets proceed

with their spin   allow handprint

on cave wall   to unearth itself

into wild-spotted horse   o news brought forth

from newborn to the un-   make and unmake

you know the drill my love   unhook me

from my body   and boil me

in your felling light

~ boil me

in your felling light

see what of my savors   weeks from now

you still need   as once by thins and pigments

you saw through   laid bare   and lapped clean

me of my garments   how the artist tastes

his admixture   the better to see it

make of me egg wash   and emulsion

by your thinning touch   braille-read me

your beauty close   as growl to ear   you remember

don't you   when I came begging

the way the sky begs   to be blue   and is

~ *if the sky begs*

to be blue and is

what it teaches   isn't rumor

but unspools in throat   the blight or burn

of psalm that begs   for everything

that isn't pleasure   bit in mouth

sun in back of eye   where light uncoils

and all those melted days   in a row

as if you were   the meat on the hook

and the hook   and I was the both-neither

the plus-minus   suited or un-

of us met and meeting   in the sunset dark

~ of us met and meeting

in the sunset dark

little is written   and less known

of our velvet slipping   down and down into

what did you call it   *your eyes on me*

our given name   spoken pitch-green

calls to us   both plus and minus

my out-breath to your in   did you hear it stutter

in your ear like a secret   no matter   what we made of it

evaporated into air   and like air kept and caught

in the lower lungs   dilating there

so I'm convinced   our prayers

are born not made

~ in back of eye our prayers

are born not made

said book on table   to river running blind

the reverse image blooms   said promise sun made

to the ocean's dark certainties   o you my body

you were born   but also made says blood

lungwise its bursting   every wish I had for

salt on my skin   utters its twin

in blueblack space   made made made

says the lost dog   to you born to flinch

or otherwise flee   o my love

I'm made of chase   and born of licking

says my singing tongue   to you the air

it's made to lick

~ you the air

I'm made to lick   since slender's the lie

we have to parse   from true   please tell me

what stays past a second   on my rough tongue

catgut-tired violin string   share with me

this burning rite   too tired to turn its head

mix this orchard fruiting   that is my love

slender on vine   tended pruned

with yours   fallow of field   temporary

as stone fruit   I took as permanent

your eyes on me   and me sky color

in your hands

~ me sky color

in your hands

me broom straw swept from room

into your wild air out and away

from all known addresses swept of fingerprint

identifying calciums into your bloodstream me

caught in catchwater and hymnody same

behind the eyelid and in the dream

of me sluicewise channel-dug downriver

by prayers washed into silty sea

me cheekbone blooming in your grove

of common milkweed me eye socket

in your field of vision o me in your field

to lay my head

~ o me in your field

to lay my head

by slipknot known   and in codicil

noted as   *wasp nest revealed by falling leaves*

by marrow to be made   pasted into sustenance

on blind tongue   slipped particulate

as stone through water   from you to be blurred

and by you removed   from the record

as in tall grasses from chaff   which echoes

and makes of its echo   a room where

curtains flutter   o me to work my way

back to your sugars   back to where sugar

~ back to where sugar

on errant tongue blooms

back to my ordinaries   boiled sweetly

on *the good eye*   movement of my arms

through salt water   *what asphalt blisters*

terrazzo cools   adumbration of hymns

gathering pine-needle thick   to accompany

coin-in-laundry jangles   back to the sloped wood

of *beach variety*'s floor   its tray of ill-fitting nails

back ghost-sugar way   after *the lunar*

to the oysters visible   under bridge at low tide

the fine hairs   of the wrist

and legs dangling high   in forty feet of ocean

a sugar drop floating   in delicate atmosphere

shimmers of what would out   barely animate then

all that would open   and these my eyes

all that would see

~ and these my eyes

that would see

and this my trace   along the fault edge

sum total of all I was   before the erasing came

and you from when   my love fit neatly

on the head of a pin   this your pinprick

on my still surface   reverberating across

an ocean held between   god's forefinger and thumb

this your oblique   pulsing with feeling

answered by these my greens   made to show

the never-was   the way water through fingers

does me imaginary   go on slipping

~ does me imaginary

go on slipping

the better to find   foothold in stone

chaffwise my beginnings   sum of your leavings

divided by tendency   to arrive late

eat in storeroom   and leave at sunrise

does me some   imaginary braid

whisper *here am i for whom   you have been waiting*

your holy vine stitched   to these my hungers

slip free of the noose   and callus-free walk

over warm stones   other than at depth

is there anywhere   I still live

as I do in the church   of your sweet mind

me untouched   and unharmed

~ me untouched and unharmed

as pulp

from orange   or *sunlight zone* undoes

its twin *twilight*   each a stillness

one gathers from the other   and petal-soft

all that stops in the throat   our singing coming

my given name and yours   one syllable

my blood and yours   one cell as if

we'd untime   reseal and make new

the scab from the skin   unhinge from nape

its thousand scars   and true

that you said of me   true

that you saw

~ true that you saw of me

you named *childlike* true

I was motion-sick and dizzy moon-sick and blind

true you named *farfetched* my last lost tooth

and green eyes moment held by fingertips gingerly

so the seam didn't tear or smoothed to nothing

as wrinkles from linen parts of me by gaze frozen

or by omission known me by bright sun blinded

girl I was shielding my eyes the better to see in you

shape of all shapes disappearing

– and you the shape

of all shapes disappearing

you the music   of all stilled songs

water of flood   into fissure sewn

neatly does it fit boxwise   all I felt

all I had to say on the matter   overflows banks

and shape it's given   impulsive to make

of all spillage new song   and new shape

prodigal hymn composed   of ashes rust

and feel of cotton   along neckline

slip of pine needles   a thousand years if a day

since your breath on my neck   these our particulars

and you islanded back   where you came from

~ these our particulars

you islanded back

those parts of me   could slip free to follow

leaguewise you   a boy in a stairwell

arms wide-flown   as his smile

and a man now   your way of talking

to pull from me   what's ugly

polish to sheen   something unreachable

or bottomless   that nonetheless

needs showing   late as late shadow

in moon-dusk   you visit me

as if every particle   held light that shuttles

out of our breathing bodies

and into another

~ that I could shuttle

out of my body

into wash of water or   like so many carbons

put to rest under shelf   of gneiss or steel

that a child should want   out of the body

away from the noise   that deep water run

both river and ocean   near enough to

my little street   easily it shuttles me

from raised voice   to hushed pew

brands on me   the spell   *I am in a body*

and wakes in me   this cobalt

by the body   am I loved

~ by this cobalt body

am I loved

cobalt sea in which my body's   bright eyespeck

obscuring a god's vision   shardwise

my own mirror   shoddy as memory

sifted thumb to forefinger   am I loved am I loved

the echoing trill   back of all songs

the crack of the ax   into new wood

and what cobalts   call me deeper

so I dive till   my lungs collapse

and you who appear there   bright eyespeck

green you correct me   *not brown*

as if I could make of you   both ax

and new wood

~ because I was both ax

and new wood

because new-matted my woolens   dew-wet my seeing

as elder or pine   both faithful and not

my good-doing   and its opposite in rhume

because yellow-tinged by tannins   the water we swam in

inland from where   the tide washed out

what channel-born bred us   sang

and held song   hymns made holy

by our tidy lungs   into new-mown grass

and by grasses known   what began us

we owned   songs that   like clockwork

slipped the body   of our shining

~ and slipped the body

all my shining

through god's loose grip fell all my wanting

from balcony at midnight limned my bit of mirror

sent high on wax wings what might've you found

those who said I was thin those who mentioned my wasting

waistwise by ropes by belt notches counted

dressed with leads made to sink all I was to tell of days

as they lengthened first star of evening

over my straw head still as the still

of tide shift at moonrise and by what god

do I mean to welcome do I mean to want

all of them all them my hungers

~ For Luke in Embryo (France 2006)

there where began   from schist and schism
the parts that shine   up from where you flaming

as when you told me

the riddle of the thousand lions   versus the sun
and I couldn't hide   my thought-exercise-smile from leaking out

there from   the cell wall in the farmhouse

from which sprang   your beating heart
where I worried over darkness   and matched step

to fox on roof   we only heard

but never saw   so in my mind it stayed   red as poppies
from schist and schism   your blue heart beating

the ocean of lions floating   light made of the same stuff

that fuels the blue-black glow   of the universe
how can it be from the moment   before the sunflowers opened

among green stalks your father   your brother

you four cells then   then eight
as the poppies their sepals   gathered then split

among the mule braying   in halflight-alarm at our approach

is that where I learned   the mica grains gather
nearby to one another in parallel   as I picked flake from roadside

for the long trip home

you among such schist   as a beating heart allows
up against all my bloodletting   as when you tell me

the riddle of the lions

how together they might   rival the sun
and I think of the poppies swaying   in the same light

as made you

~ *Redux (Borrowed Thing)*

no one told you   the way a painting's   a box with breath-holes suited
to unstated need   no one said   the borrowed thing flitting
past your eye   owns the part of your heart   that sucks in the blood
no one warned about   a piercing blue   in morning sky being
the root of some   existential disharmony   no telling beforehand
the spectrum of particularities   in the mower's hum   *several sounds*
interacting   with the breathing-box singing   on wall
makes you drop back   to the day at Redux you
picked him up   laid it wet on the seat   watched your corners
till off peninsula   and safely past   where the firemen   *nine*
in sofa store   died that year   then looked and saw
everything he didn't say   on his face   no one told you   past your eye
in daylight   you'd record hummingbird so long   he's late to practice
the sky being   the root of it   from whence mysteries   emerge and return

emerge and return   like song   the man on the radio   explaining that pleasure

is fleeting   *so we survive longer*   *so we are always trying*   borne out by science

this thing you know   to the breathing box   say nothing

to the borrowed thing   don't let on

~ *Came My Own Sunlight*

came my own sunlight   down and down shattering
came glass from my own   silvered breaking

came my beginnings flush   to their foretellings

and in ash came ash   volcanoes from my deep-under
came utterances   lowing from the belly

came foretold deaths   and their light

a comet's tail after burning   came afterburns on skin
and their scars   came bruises turned blue then yellow

& came all manner of blueing

along with blue singing   came the unhinging of doors
came locks springing open   and all the yellows of spring

came the scent of daffodils

into a room of sleeping babes   came a bomb
with my name on it   and bullet same

came my name in the hymnal

mine among a dozen   jawbones arrayed upwards to sky
came my identifying carbons   and the counting of ribs

came issuing from me   my confessions

out and out like a river   the banks can't hold
did all of them flow   those I'd hit with sticks

those I'd coveted   when least they needed coveting

o room of sleeping babes   o children everywhere sleeping
came your grey eyes then   came your blues

to me as if   all had been real

and from what scattered   a whole could form
from this hard clay came you   came me still living

~ *Blue Bottle*

The story in which one girl walks with another

on the beach and finds a blue bottle.

One finds the bottle mesmerizing the other

spell-breaking by nature says yes beautiful

but leave it here.

And with one gesture saves both their lives.

Leave the bottle here. When the time comes

I will talk us out of it the one thinks but doesn't say. By the time

the time comes the bottle is half broken and the one

does what she says and finds a way. The dune

a blanched line by then the water

a good option if you're a strong swimmer.

Turns out she is a girl

who doesn't save her own skin. If she knew it before

she didn't know she knew. The bottle still beautiful by half.

Both their lives in that one thing.

Leave it here.

When the time comes I will talk us out of it.

~ convince me songbird

and I'll go easily

tell me your singing takes you   into the *not not*

and I'll chalk to nothing   what my mother called *plenty*

I'll on its face count   as at least a thousand denials

the eyeblink   that spiraled inside me for years

you can't hear it but   it's willful   the turn at the bridge

where I admit   it's not a sin   to go easily into melody

do it now   try telling me to want otherwise   and you'll find

down from trees as well as   out on the naked branch

at the appointed hour   my greens abiding all others

songbird   look deep into   my own *not not*

for a note's rest   and from it go toward

what did my mother call it   of the ten thousand things

she counted four   the blue sky   don't add to it

us at the cars   and me singing close to your ear

but count twice the vireo   obsessed with clouds

its too-high *not not*   count at least that you *did* look

that you tried to hear me   and I'll string cloth from the eaves

call surrender on   finding your blues

exactly where I left them   songbird   by way of alarm

or faint praise   convince me   we are *not* meant

by blue of our sky   or blue of song

and not made   by means of one another

to open the throat

~ *open your throat and sing*

so was prophet girl told

as it closes *so does it open* so said something to her

from its high place down down to asphalt

so does it open that held close by mishap

is she misshapen and by tides ruled

nothing to tempt her like open blossom within earshot

of wings supersonic and so what if her shape' s made for closing

by gunshot or hymn to learn melody so does she open

so sings she hands at middle folded in choir practice

if she's a rattling chain all around her the sound opens

so says the prophet girl like blood's own becoming

equal parts iron and oxygen slipping unfurled as petal

into heat till almost rubbed to nothing you know

the type says prophet girl to anyone with her same thirst

if not an open mouth then closed yes hummingbird

chooses feeder   or ready bloom whichever   if she's

a straight arrow   she closes distance to target   and all *is* closed

no   not everything   is there an easy way   to learn it

once open the petals   what seemed at first closed   just needs

the lock tried   what folds unfolds   yes eventually   but

she's burned   isn't she burned   by the sound

of all that opening   *it can't close back*   *or it* won't *close*

so she says   so says the prophet girl

acknowledgments

All my days I'll live inside a deep, almost bottomless gratitude to Wesleyan University, and Wesleyan University Press, most especially Suzanna Tamminen, who saw in these poems an inner light I scarcely could see, then kept that light central to the editorial project. One could not ask for more in an editor, or in a friend. Thank you.

At Fairfield University, I thank Richard Greenwald, Nicole Heller, Phil Klay, Karen Osborn, Elizabeth Petrino, Christine Siegel, and Emily Smith, each of whom by their friendship, example, or commitment to their own searching lived these poems with me over a number of years, whether they knew it or not. Others lived these poems without knowing it all over town, reminding me to stay in and with the present moment in all its complexity. Thank you therefore to Twyla, Nick, Andre, Donald, David, Mandy, Amy, Heidi, Kate, Curt, Jane, Curtis, Brady, Eli, Johnny, and Josh.

A songbird sings the song it is first taught. This song has been a lifetime in the making, and so I would like to acknowledge that brave and merry band who was present at the beginning: my parents, my sister, and my five brothers. Your love first formed in me a wonder for all that is majestic in ourselves and the world.

And to my husband Garrett and our sons Willem and Luke: you remain all and everything always.

about the author

Carol Ann Davis is the author of the poetry collections *Psalm* (2007) and *Atlas Hour* (2011) and the essay collection *The Nail in the Tree* (2020), all published by Tupelo Press. She is a professor of English at Fairfield University, where she is director of the Low-Residency MFA and founding director of Poetry in Communities, an initiative that brings writing workshops to communities hit by sudden or systemic violence. Recipient of a National Endowment for the Arts fellowship in Poetry and finalist for the National Magazine Award in Essays and Criticism, she has published work in a number of magazines and journals, including *The Atlantic, The Daily Beast, The Georgia Review, Image, The Gettysburg Review,* and *The American Poetry Review.*